This Notebook Belongs To:

....

....

....

Made in the USA
Las Vegas, NV
10 June 2023

73248650R00061